Jean Vanier

Terry Barber

ACTIVIST SERIES

Jean Vanier is published by
Grass Roots Press, a division of Literacy Services of Canada Ltd.

PHONE 1–888–303–3213
WEBSITE www.grassrootsbooks.net

ACKNOWLEDGMENTS

We thank L'Arche Canada for supplying the majority of the photographs.
For more information, visit the L'ARCHE™ website at www.larche.ca.
L'ARCHE™ is a trade-mark owned by L'Arche Canada and used under license.

We acknowledge the financial support of the Government of Canada through the Book Publishing Industry Development Program (BPIDP) for our publishing activities.

We acknowledge the support of
the Alberta Foundation for the Arts
for our publishing programs.

Editor: Dr. Pat Campbell
Consultant: Beth Porter, L'Arche Canada
Image research: Dr. Pat Campbell
Book design: Lara Minja, Lime Design Inc.

Library and Archives Canada Cataloguing in Publication

Barber, Terry, date
    Jean Vanier / Terry Barber.

ISBN 978-1-894593-86-1

    1. Vanier, Jean, 1928- 2. Arche (Association) 3. Group homes for people with disabilities. 4. Church work with people with disabilities. 5. Catholics—Canada—Biography. 6. Readers for new literates. I. Title.

PE1126.N43B36454 2008   428.6'2   C2008-901993-8

Printed in Canada

Contents

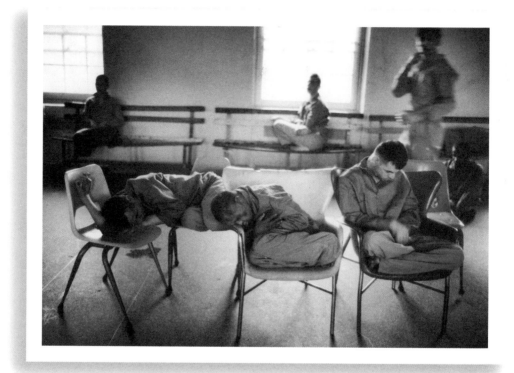

These people live in an institution.

Being Human

It is 1964. Many people with disabilities have hard lives. They are kept behind closed doors. They are kept apart from others. They are not part of the community. Their lives are dull. Every day is the same for them.

Many people with disabilities live in **institutions**.

Jean Vanier makes friends with people who have
intellectual disabilities.

Being Human

Human beings want to love. Human beings want to be loved. Many people with disabilities are not loved. Without love, people feel less human. In 1964, a man makes life better for people with disabilities. His name is Jean Vanier.

"…being human is to be a friend to the weak person."

– *Jean Vanier*

Jean and his brothers.

Jean sits with his
brothers and sister.

Early Years

Jean Vanier is born in 1928. He has three brothers and a sister. Jean's parents are Catholic. They are religious. Jean's family prays together every day. Jean's parents like to help others. Jean learns that helping others is important.

Jean is born in Switzerland.

Jean and his family in England.

Front row: Jean and his brothers and sister.
Back row: Jean's nanny, Jean's father and mother,
the nanny's niece.

Early Years

Jean's parents are Canadian. His father works for the government of Canada. He is a **diplomat.** He serves Canada in different countries. Jean grows up in England. In 1939, Jean's family moves to France. Jean is 11 years old.

Jean learns to speak French and English.

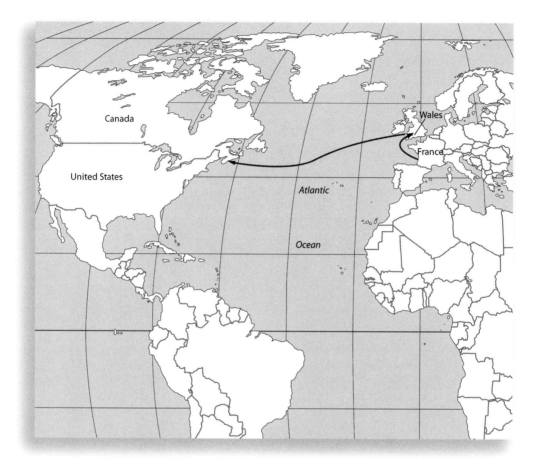

Jean travels from France to Canada.

Early Years

World War II starts in 1939. It is not
safe to live in France. Many people
want to leave France. The Vaniers
leave France in 1940. Jean takes a ship
to Canada. Jean's brother and sisters
go with him.

This poster shows sailors in the British navy.

Jean Joins the Navy

It is 1942. Jean wants to help with the war. He wants to join the British Navy. He tells his father. Jean's father says "I trust you." These words show that Jean's father believes in him. These words mean a lot to Jean.

Jean wants to work for peace.

A German ship fires on an Allied ship.

Jean Joins the Navy

Jean travels to England by ship. He is only 13 years old. It is dangerous to travel during the war. The Germans want to sink **Allied** ships. Jean is lucky. He arrives safely in England. He begins navy college.

Jean takes a train to the ship.

Jean in his
navy uniform.

Jean and his
classmates,
1945.

Jean Joins the Navy

Jean studies at college. The war ends in 1945. Jean becomes an officer. He transfers to the Canadian Navy. At age 21, Jean leaves the navy. He wants to find the meaning of his life. He meets a wise priest named Father Thomas.

Jean asks Father Thomas to be his spiritual father.

Jean Vanier in 1952.

Jean Searches for Meaning

Jean begins a life of prayer and study. He tries to understand the meaning of life. He is not sure what he wants to do with his life. Jean goes to university. He works hard. Jean gets his **Ph.D** in 1962.

Jean gets his degree from the Catholic University of Paris.

Jean
teaches
ethics.

Jean teaches at the University of Toronto.

Jean Searches for Meaning

Jean moves to Canada. He gets a job at a university. He loves to teach. The students love his classes. But Jean wants something more. Jean believes in social justice. Jean begins to visit people with disabilities.

Father Thomas takes Jean to visit people in institutions.

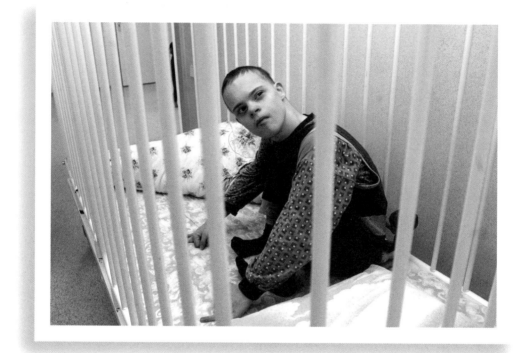

A person with an intellectual disability sits in a caged bed.

Jean Searches for Meaning

Jean meets many people with disabilities. They want to be Jean's friends. Jean sees how they live. They are not treated like humans. They are locked up, like criminals. Jean feels sad. He wants people with disabilities to have better lives.

Jean's house in France, 1964.

Jean Searches for Meaning

Jean leaves his teaching job. He returns to France in 1964. He buys a house in a village. He asks two men to live with him. These men have disabilities. Their lives get better in their new home. Jean has found his **calling.**

Noah builds an ark to save God's creatures from the flood.

L'Arche

The three men form a special community.
Jean names the community "L'Arche".
The name "L'Arche" is French for "The
Ark." In the Bible, the ark is a **symbol** of
safety. The ark is also a symbol for hope.

Father
Thomas helps
to form
L'Arche.

The L'Arche family grows.

L'Arche

The L'Arche community begins to grow. L'Arche opens more homes. More people move into the L'Arche homes. Some of the village people help in the homes. These people are called assistants. The assistants' lives change. They find more meaning in their lives.

People come from different countries to help in the homes.

A L'Arche home in Canada, 1971.

L'Arche

The L'Arche community keeps growing. L'Arche homes begin to open in many countries. In 1971, Jean helps to start a new group. It is called "Faith and Light." This group supports families who have children with disabilities.

Jean visits a Faith and Light group in Madagascar. Today, there are about 1,500 groups around the world.

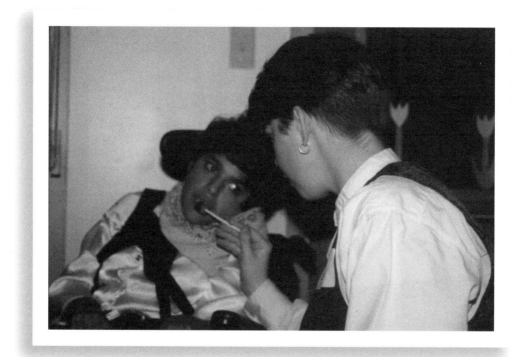

An assistant helps a L'Arche member to taste a new food.

L'Arche

In L'Arche, people with disabilities are called **core** members. They teach the assistants about loving and forgiving. They teach the assistants about being human.

The assistants help the core members with their needs. Some core members cannot eat on their own. The assistants help them.

Jean says, "The people with disabilities are my teachers."

L'Arche members make lunch together.

L'Arche

The core members have full lives. They have friends. They trust one another. They feel safe. They learn new skills. They learn to cook. They learn how to do crafts. Some get a job. The core members feel safe to grow and learn.

L'Arche members bake together.

Jean and Marc share a cup of tea.

L'Arche

The L'Arche members live in a home. They live together like a family. The L'Arche members like to spend time together. They talk about their day. They share their day over a cup of tea. They invite other people to share a meal with them.

L'Arche members celebrate Christmas.

L'Arche

The L'Arche members love to celebrate. They celebrate with music. They celebrate with food.

The L'Arche members like to pray. They thank God for their lives. They thank God for one another. They thank God for all their blessings.

L'Arche members respect their different religions.

Letu and Robin share a happy moment.

L'Arche

L'Arche is based on love and respect. Core members learn self-respect. They feel valued. Assistants feel valued. They all learn about their gifts. Many core members have a special gift. The special gift is their ability to accept others as they are.

Jean gives a talk.

Jean Spreads Hope

Today, Jean still lives in the first L'Arche community. He travels around the world. He talks about hope. He talks about caring for one another. Jean Vanier is a Canadian who **inspires** the world. He has made the world a better place.

Jean gets the Order of Canada.

Glossary

Allied: relating to the nations that fought against Germany and other countries in World War II.

calling: an inner urge to pursue an activity.

core: the central part.

diplomat: a person who represents a government in its relations with other governments.

ethics: moral standards.

institution: a place that provides care for people with disabilities.

inspire: to encourage somebody to do something.

intellectual disability: an impaired ability to learn.

Ph.D.: these three letters mean Doctor of Philosophy.

symbol: something that stands for an idea.

Talking About the Book

What did you learn about Jean Vanier?

What did you learn about L'Arche?

Jeans says: "being human is to be a friend to the weak person." What does "being human" mean to you?

Jeans says: "The people with disabilities are my teachers." What do you think Jean learns from people with disabilities?

How has Jean Vanier made the world a better place?

Picture Credits